Corner Office

D1565627

Also By Susan Hahn

NOVELS

Losing Beck
The Six Granddaughters of Cecil Slaughter

POETRY

The Note She Left
The Scarlet Ibis
Self/Pity
Mother In Summer
Holiday
Confession
Melancholia, et cetera
Incontinence
Harriet Rubin's Mother's Wooden Hand

PLAYS

The Scarlet Ibis
Golf

Corner Office

Poems by Susan Hahn

Word Poetry

Published by Word Poetry
P.O. Box 541106
Cincinnati, OH 45254-1106

ISBN: 9781625494542

Poetry Editor: Kevin Walzer
Business Editor: Lori Jareo

Visit us on the web at www.wordpoetrybooks.com

Remembering Mark Strand

his genius, his kindness

Everything you can imagine is real.

Pablo Picasso

Most think of me as inanimate—
certainly not capable of emotion.
This is how I've been drawn
in fiction, science, and poems.

Anyway, that's how it's been—
and I suppose will always be.
So much more about them—
what they feel, what they see.

Here, at least, I get a section—
my perception, my story—
my view
in all its done-in glory.

Earth

Table of Contents

First Wall

Earth

There was a moment
where I had everything
arranged. The furniture
perfect—the space enormous
and elegant.
But once they started
pillaging and setting fires, smashing
invaluable objects
(the weighted Buddha
marble statue;
the Klimt painting—
the bliss on the woman's face,
the man's anchored—so certain—embrace,
how the gold
leaf mingled with the oil paint;
the Byzantine glass
that composed the lamp's light)
and shredding the plans
laid out so neatly
on my desk,

(continued, no stanza break)

14

I just ran and watched
from a distance.
The pain—that deep love ache of attachment—
too much. And yes, there too,
was the double electric
fence from Auschwitz—
one of the more recent grotesque objects,
positioned near a bulging closet—
no more room in the tribal rooms, family rooms,
or the ones for costumes.
The junk just keeps piling up.

Then I thought a change,
a different prayer,
might help. Another god—a new face
than those I was used to—
might pull me back,
hold me to what was supposed to be
my place.

Man

I remember her body—
most precisely
her breasts
when she put
one on each side of my face.
How they made me overlook
my world mess. Blinders
or dream pillows that soothed
my blistered mind
so that all facts,
all hypotheses, all thoughts,
all gossip

about the fellow
who took my space
would evaporate and I would be left
with just softness,
until a strength

between my legs grew

(continued, no stanza break)

and it didn't matter who
"she" was. I'd plunge
myself into her—however anonymous.

Often now, I fall out of orbit,
especially at the moment of full wakefulness,
and am impaled with a rage
not toward whoever she is
who lies next to me,
but the rat
who politicked and won
the corner office that
I lost.

Then I focus
on the faraway woman
who could calm.
How in the aftermath of loss
I abruptly ran

away to what
I hoped would be
a warmer climate,

(continued, no stanza break)

to forget.

***

That has not yet happened.

Woman

Make me turn off the reality
TV I can't stop watching.
I've become a voyeur of staged life
to distract myself from the tumult
caused by his cold exit.

Lead me to a candlelit room
with a thick, cream colored carpet,
a large bed with as yet unspotted
sheets of the highest thread count.

We could stay there forever
far above the city—
our silky love a supple robe
wrapped around us both.

On my low, tiny balcony
I cry to the blotchy sky:

(continued, stanza break)

Remember Me. Remember Us.

What Exactly Is Any Of This About?

Man

She was too much
a romantic.
It became ridiculous.
Anyway, the growth
on my mind grew too large over
the loss of my corner office.

I remember one night
while working late
a migrating bird lost its way,
mistook my lights for the stars,
and smashed
into the huge slab of window glass.

What a mess.

I am *that*
disoriented.

Woman

I pray each night that he'll change—
spin only around me.
The phone will ring and he'll be
the complete
distraction

from the chaos—
the explosives tossed
into random crowds,
the planned beheadings.

Who gives us all this consciousness
—conscience?—
then slowly sucks or quickly snatches
it away?

***

Aggrieved, I sought a different temple,
a new book, but it didn't
(continued, no stanza break)

help—its word-path
impossibly simple.

The old philosophers are of no use.
They do not know this new world,
could not imagine its texts—
the quickness of electronic clutter—
decipher neither the benign
nor malignant chatter.

Earth

The new prayer,
although less garish,
did not nourish more
than the last and yet
I said a prayer for it—
the one more delicate.
And while I prayed
I let my lessened power drift
and mourned it.

But at the *Amen* the sick feeling
returned full force
and I found myself getting
even further off course.

Second Wall

Earth

I cannot seem to stop
the injuries inflicted
upon my surface
unless I throw myself
completely out of orbit.
A suicide
of sorts to end the damage—
the noise and drill
into my scalp.

I fantasize the aftermath—
the quiet, the untethered
floating. A silhouette upon
which some astronomer or poet
from a young, well-tended planet
would become transfixed
enough to study, marvel over,
then to write about....

Man

The movers bubble-wrapped
my chairs—thirty years
of upholstered rears sitting there,
their fronts facing me. The firm
telling me if I ever return
to "say hello" I could have a cubicle,
if I first would email.

Now, I need more than one
woman to soothe me as I begin
my leave
of this planet.
Here, if I choose
I can have seven different pairs
of breasts in one week—new moons
circling my face. The online hook-up sites
are addictive. It's true

she was my Sunday best,
even now, with her voice

                    (continued, no stanza break)

across the dead miles
still a spiral in my head.
But since the eclipse
of losing my corner office
she was not enough.

(*I know* in my older age
I am becoming
 redundant.)

Being reborn into the church helps.
The weekend potlucks—
the women salty, round, and generous.

Hungry…

Although none speaks like she—
her leaps and pirouettes
of thought so curious—a poet.

Woman

I write and peek
at my Caller
ID. All ringers off.
I need quiet,
the safety of silence—
that thin tissue
which holds the words
and the world so fragile.
Here, others' scissors and snipes
cannot cut into
the patterns I create.

Daytime, when the sun is too bright—
florid with a high noon
disease—it melts my eyes
to blur and tears
as if there were a rage
in its glare—my father

standing over me, his stare

(continued, no stanza break)

29

as if I can do nothing
right. Although now that's impossible,
for he just shuffles from bed to chair,
then in reverse...

A hearse awaits.

Earth

Once I was in love
with myself. My passion
the mountains, their peaks—
each an orgasmic high.
The oceans rumbled bravado,
the rivers and the creeks ruffled
and the green and yellow weeds
rolled with the breeze to rhythmic delight.

Now, parts of me are so greasy—
an oily bowel sludge I cannot wipe
away. There isn't a brook clean enough,
while my other parts are so dry—
an eczema I've scratched to blood
which matches other pools of it
that cover me.
What a sour, sorry color.

I ask, "How did it come to this?"
There was a desert and some wanderers
(continued, no stanza break)

surviving the elements, getting stronger.

Now, I am left staring
into the obliterated
glass of another broken into
office, my shattered
reflection a reminder—

I saw the two planes heading in....

Man

I'll call her tomorrow.
Invite her to visit.
Hope she's changed her mind—
is inclined to incline
her body next to me,
allow there to be
no questions asked.

My life has changed so much.

Soon the boxes will arrive.
The furniture—the chairs
so meticulously crafted.
The best.
Like her breasts.

After she leaves, I'll go back
to my "weekday" bodies.
It's no secret.
I aim for directness,

(continued, stanza break)

but am also fond of subtext

and do love some leaps of faith.

Now, I accept the wafer

as His body.

Yet, her echo haunts:

Remember Me. Remember Us.

What Exactly Is Any Of This About?

My answer as I grow old:

The Church. Her Breasts. Memories

Of My Corner Office.

Woman

Once I had a corner office.
But before I moved into it—
after my promotion—
it was sliced in half,
right down the center,
split like the vagina is,
because unlike my predecessor
I didn't have a penis.

It overlooked a gravel roof,
and the view from its windows
was a clogged grey,
because a higher storied, moldy
building submerged most of the sky
with its soot and smoke.

Especially on that September day....

Third Wall

Woman

Although I didn't have a world view
I liked what I saw from my sliced in two
corner office, its large, smudged window—
the gravel that covered the adjacent roof
a half-floor down.
How a misguided pigeon
would take a stone into its beak,
thinking it was something good to eat.
A hard reminder of what I would swallow—

the times he refused to speak to me
from across the kitchen table, just chewing
on a chunk of meat,
or something I had said.

(Our complete story inconsequential—
its minutiae floating on the westward wind
toward two as yet unopened graves.)

However, I did thrive on the small "hellos"
                        (continued, no stanza break)

and "good nights" from the other workers.
Although most of the nourishment arrived
with the man who worked the night shift.
He must have chosen it (or was it force-fed
to him?) for skin grafts so raw
covered his face.
A troubled world map.
(What unforeseen devastation
had he walked into?)

He always gave
me the grandest smile,
while we'd talk in earnest about the erratic
weather—the extremes of heat, then cold,
mixing up the vegetation, the flowers' confusion.

I'd look forward to the sight of him
at my door, his large bin filled
with the day's trash.
Both of us so mottled.
He on the outside, I within.

I miss him—his straightforwardness.

(continued, no stanza break)

Different from how I miss he who lives

across the miles—

the tunnels underneath our talk.

The times he was in angry bass

voice and I in my weak, pathetic—

or bitch operatic.

Tonight, I wonder if he misses me—not

the man on the edge

of an opposite, unsettled ocean,

but the man so dappled.

His grace a class

to be studied.

Earth

I fell in love once
with a faraway star—and began
to give it all my focus.

I was drugged and dumbed and euphoric
as love does—filled with a lovely, light
anesthesia.
So discouraged, so heavy
from the doings on me—the excrement
smeared and thick—
it was only my clean, faraway star,
almost beyond my reach—
its twinkle and shine—
that brightened me, made me feel
less nauseous.

So pure. So simple. So distant.
The allure of its constancy unbelievable.

***

Eventually it began to dim—
as I know all stars do—
and I found it hard to find.
My obsessive squint and strain searching
to see it, too painful.

After this, I became less attached
to anything, except, perhaps, myself.

***

Loss does this.

Man

Tonight the woman's breasts were too small
to fall softly against my cheeks.
I pulled at them so they might
until she shrieked.
She grew more excited
by such pain, so I did it again
and again.

Last night the woman's breasts were large enough
but too hard with implants,
as was she, in all her full
self-glory.

Tomorrow I will call *her*
and she will answer only the phone,
not the question
I will ask:
"May I come *there* for a visit?"

She'll call what I want

            (continued, no stanza break)

"An Inconsequential Moment Of No Substance."

***

Sentimental. Quixotic. Diaphanous. Damn. Poet.

I want to erase her from my mind.
An erasure *NOW.*
Not what we all come to
in our own scrubbed-out time.

Earth

I wish I could have stayed
as I was in my prime.
Who doesn't? As it is
with everyone, I want
my pastures back.
No bald or balding spots.

I loved the seasons—
how they embraced me all
at once in their range
of temperature and color.
How I adored my body.

Now I weep a lot over my rot.

Self-pity?

Why Not?

Man

Nine large boxes arrived
today and in four of them,
carefully wrapped,
my fine chairs.
I sat in each and stared
at my cardboard life.

The widow from across the way
came over with a casserole
and we ate. Then satisfied—
her bloated stomach doubling
over her worn underpants,
as did mine—
we satisfied ourselves again.
Afterward, I turned my back to her—
her side yeasty and a rumpled mess—
and she left

with her oven bake, empty dish.
I thought I heard her plywood door
(continued, no stanza break)

slam shut—the splintering of its wood—
even from a distance.

I'll sleep with her again next week,
although at this minute
she'd deny it, so filled she is
with the pothole of disgust.
I, too, know of *that.*

She senses—with woman sense—
there's another for whom I pine—
that joy-voice bouncing
off the cellphone towers.

***

For now, I'll unpack
my two clocks, accounting books,
five old expensive pens—
still elegant as my once young man penis.
My life so ripe and steady then
as was my hand, which now has a slight,
but noticeable shake, except

(continued, no stanza break)

when I hold on to a warm, accepting breast.

The diagnosis could have been
worse—the beginnings
of Parkinson's, Alzheimer's, a tumor.
I know—for now—I am blessed

with just my Benign Essential Tremor,
my boxes to sort through, and my thoughts
of her voice—harmless pings igniting
the secretive, explosive desert.

Woman

He called last night, his voice a *faux*
upbeat. We didn't speak of breasts or visits.
Maybe he already knows
I cannot give
into the condition he presents, to live
only in the present.
Yet, he made me feel so present
I forgot my father who now only exists
lying down, his eyes half open—
his view so dim.
His arms wrapped in gauze
because his skin is so thin
it can tear from any movement.

Instead, he spoke about a book
he was reading on terrorism.
I stayed quiet—frightened—
and didn't ask
how he felt about the pieces
of his life being returned
(continued, no stanza break)

to him.

***

Tomorrow I'll attend the Shabbat service.
Pray for both of them, although
my Judaism is a poorly fruited tree
of little nourishment.

And with the emailed selection
of this week's Torah portion to be discussed:

"Jacob's daughter Dina is raped
by the son of the neighboring chief,
and her brothers take revenge
by murdering all the men of that city."

my only thought:
how is *this* supposed to help?

* **

On twilight's sharp-edged eve—
(continued, no stanza break)

before I take my final leave—
I am trying to figure all of it out
so I can carry it with me—
a soft pillow curved fetal
between my breasts and knees.

Fourth Wall

Man

I am hip. I am hot.
I like the rotation of women
around me. To them I am
the sun when I show up.

At the precipice of old
I am grateful for the new
medicines and mores.
The casualness of sex
without any casualties.
But sometimes

inside my stucco bungalow,
counting my condoms,
I still feel so absolutely alone.
A conundrum.
And it's then I pick up
the phone, call her, call
anyone.

Woman

Stupidity is not my strong suit.
Although I wear it rather well,
for when I see his number
on my Caller ID I quickly pick it up.
Then I feel sick from the over-
excitement—and the hopelessness.

***

I understand his fixating on
perfect breasts—his way
of coping with, among other things,
early mother-loss.
Yet I feel I can no longer be
her substitute—
or his therapist.

Earth

We are all a bunch of emigrants—
particles moving through the vapor.
Looking for the place called *"Mother."*

So fouled are we from others' feet,
trying to get to that safe place,
when in our hearts' depth
we know *She's* already been
and left—or never was, in fact.
I don't know

if I ever knew
where to go or what to do,
even though I sometimes
present myself as
both *worldly* and *earthy.*

Sorry for the puns.
But sometimes a little word-
play tipples me out of orbit,

(continued, no stanza break)

allows me to forget

my place—my own time in the line....

Man

Tonight, after I rested inside
a worn woman—not entirely
worn out—I noticed her
furniture, quite modern.
Studied its youthfulness.

I like the space between
the unadorned spindles on her chairs.
Her dresser, spare and functional—
its wide, deep drawers,
the unfussy fabric of her shades.

She is not like the faraway one—
her questions always popping like a thumb
pushing on the bubble wrap of my newly arrived
possessions: memories of passions,
deals done, the laughter
of voices heard.

Hers.

Earth

The sun is getting too bright,
a fever to it,
causing me to become too
high-pitched.
I am dizzy and losing weight.
My skin peels off
certain parts. Others are mud-
clumps turning into mud-
swamps from the violent rains,
severing the heads of trees.

No one lives lightly on me.

I dream of scouring myself clean—
on my knees with a holy-
stone as a sailor does
his ship. Then *I* could sail away
to find and please my lost star—

or at least one similar.

(continued, stanza break)

I want my lust and luster back.
But I am going in reverse—aged
with my head bent over into the sunk
of my neck. My balance a slow
vertigo. My belly a bloat.

My veins punctured and bruised
from the polluted, intravenous fluids.

Woman

I've begun to pick at myself
again, mark my body
with pinpricks of loneliness.
The ingrown hairs—small worms—
have once more burrowed
into my thighs
and need to be excised.
I need

to extract him.
His thick penis
pulled out.
This midnight hour,

does it push into another?

***

Long ago my skin sloughed off.
An allergic reaction to something
(continued, no stanza break)

61

I swallowed.

Yet, however much the layers

of dermis burned away,

at the end of months

of the relentless

healing itch,

I looked brand new.

Luck. Returned

to baby innocence. Way before

his polluted tongue and ego

is where I want to travel.

Cleansed. A Baptism.

Earth

When I itch I cannot help but scratch.
I am as impulsive as the rest—
they who repulsively gorge
upon my body.
The only balm is *memory*—
my faraway star.

(That's what the doctors told
the dying old man when he asked,
"What NOW
should I think about?"

Their answer: "Good Thoughts Past.")

Man

I called her today,
told her about the boxes—
their arrival. How difficult
it was to open them—
my life wrapped up
in old news-
papers, traveling to me
across the used up
decades.

Then I laughed and she did too,
and how fully fleshed I felt,
remembering our bed
and how sometimes all motion
and conversation came together.

My life is not yet over…

Woman

I forgot my emptiness
as I did a little
dance around the room,
cellphone in hand—
magic wand.

The Earth's vertigo—
especially of late—
became a spin of an early
1960's Sinatra song with me
in three crinolines
of various poof
beneath my brightly patterned
polished cotton summer skirt.
My white cotton underpants holding tight
a mound of yet unopened secrets.
The sing-song menace of noise
in my head not fully birthed.

I was so young—a lovely cliché—

(continued, no stanza break)

and Death could easily be
pushed away.
Yes, I dipped and swayed
to memories not quite lost,

although much of the talk
was about objects boxed.

Floor

Woman

My father is now in hospice care.
He is in his 104th year.
When visitors are expected
the attendants rouge
his cheeks a bit and loosely wrap
a soft scarf of lavender, peach, and apricot
around his neck.
The colors so pleasant.

His name is "Sol."
In Spanish, "El Sol." The Sun.
All my life I've spun around him
to try to get a little
attention. A crumb.

He counts to 10
when in too much pain.

1 2 3 4 5 6 7 8 9 10

(continued, stanza break)

Then starts over again....
I listen to the din
of his voice—a train of 10
cars fading into the distance,
then reappearing at the fogged-up station.

***

Soon in the dark—
the heaviness of night pushing down
on me—I'll press
into my fantasies
about the man who hints
he's coming for a visit.

Sadly, his view is all

there is, all there will be,
as it is with many
too passionate
love stories—violent, then silent.
There will never be any permanency.
                    (continued, stanza break)

Especially from the fantasy
of an overheated place
high above the city.
Its floor an unyielding hard oak
underneath the thick, inviting carpet.

Earth

When I saw *her*
writing in her corner
I could not help
but remember my fading
faraway star.

Igniting herself
only with her pen,
she then flickers out again.

1 2 3 4 5 6 7 8 9 10

I hear him, too,
even though his counting is now
almost inaudible,
just small, spaced breaths.
No more decibels...

the music of death.

Man

I'm almost done—
down to
the bric-a-brac and bobbleheads.
Soon they will be placed—
these cheap extraneous pieces
that made up so much of my life—
on obscure shelves or in large junk drawers
I've cleared for them.
"Organization" was the motto
of my large section. And, yes,
I was once considered
a great success.

And no, *I am not yet boxed.*
I feel it, the call
to her showed me
this. My penis rose
high as we talked.
It just happened—no pill taken.

                          (continued, stanza break)

I went to church,
then bought a ticket
to travel East.
Lay with her.
Lie to her. Returned
to the West, I'll sit
in the lattice cabinet
and confess.

Woman

My father's corner office
always faced the full moon,
a quarter or a half
not good enough.

He hoped for a son—a replication
of himself. When he got
an edited version
his own face became his whole
focus. The moon a mere reflection
of his own.

                ***

The night he died
all that was left was
bone and an oily stain,
spoiled and fetal,
on his white, fitted sheet—
that blank space where

                        (continued, no stanza break)

74

inside a poem exists.

I picked a casket of oak—
I think. Didn't ask, just pointed
to it. And a dark silk
tie for him that looked fine enough
for an ambassador travelling
to a foreign country,
trying to make
a good impression
on a higher-up
dignitary.

***

I heard the thud
when they shut his vault.
His office now
with no view,
not even to the winter's mud.

Man

I've not yet seen her—
her father's death a doorstop.
So I continue to rotate
the women here.
Eclipse their bodies
with my heft and moan.
It makes me forget my own
approaching death.

My corner office
fully unpacked blends well
with the other items
I've purchased. I tell myself
it's quite good enough.

Yet, across the false
quiet of the desert,
before blank sleep's solution,
I curve around her
and, again, the tornadic spin
of more life comes...

Woman

He left a message
asking how I am.
How am I? I asked
the mirror. It replied
with a stare
of reproach for my intrusion.
As if *it* could know
me better than I do.
Which it does,
just from its look.

I feel nothing for the moment
or the before or after.
I am numb.
My father in the ground—
it's minus two outside—
his too thin bones now frozen,
wearing his grey suit and that blue tie.

***

I like his question
How are you? – its lace
of concern for me—
and wonder if my mother
has realized that her man
now lies next to her
on that bottomed-out floor.

Maybe he, too, said:
How are you?
as he was lowered next to her
into what now is

that subzero bed.

Earth

Only a few consider
how I am.
Most do a dervish dance
around me—"The Busy."
Its steps a quick iPod jog—
a plugged-in fix—
a fast distraction
from the dirge-taunt
of the grave. While each day
I become more off key,
align myself with the dying
—the small notes on the dim sheet
music of their lives,
or their encounters with unexpected,
cacophonous horrors.

Man

She hasn't returned
my many calls
and as I wait
I shuffle
my papers. Refile
my life.

Here, the weather remains
warm and bright
with the grass in different stages of life
from parched to verdant—
the well-placed clouds,
their shapes reminders
of the bodies I've caressed.

I think of her—
the constant wonder
if I'll ever again see her face,
or if she, too, has disappeared
like my corner office.

Ceiling

Woman

The image of my father's newly dug
open grave next to my mother's
mud-encrusted vault
has taken away most other thoughts.

I've stripped myself bare,
sit in my chair with my pen and paper,
deleting
words that are
superfluous.

I've decided not
to call him, or anyone, but to exist
not inside the clutter of others' thoughts,
or corner offices and those who mourn them.

Rather

to live long within
the open field
of a poem.

Man

Live long within
the open field
of a poem?!?

Earth

Yes. Live long within
the open field
of a poem.

Sky

Earth

Sometimes I dream
I float inside the old temples,
viewing their mosaic ceilings—
their told stories a blaze from above.
They raise me up
to where I believe

I could drift in white space
for eons—
become myself

a poem.